ON THE FARM

GW01398652

Diane James & Sara Lynn

Illustrated by Siobhan Dodds

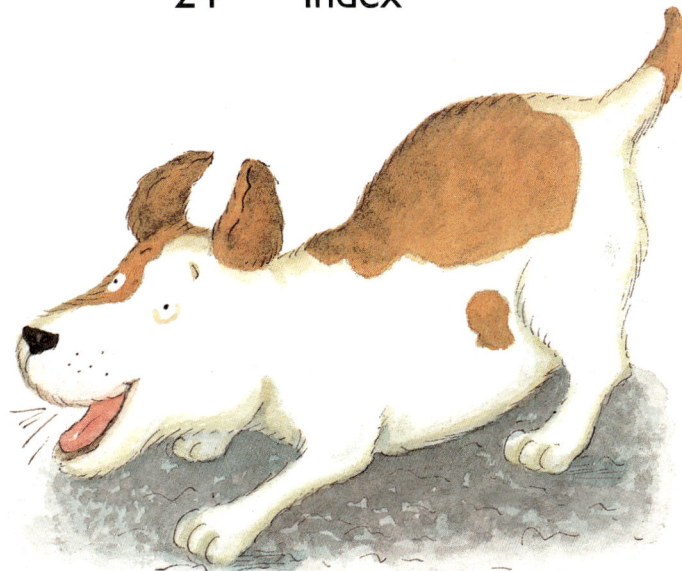

TWO-CAN

Have you ever visited a farm? Most farm animals are kept because they provide milk, eggs and meat. Some are kept as family pets. Farmers have to work very hard. Every day they feed all the animals and make sure they have water to drink. The cows have to be milked and eggs collected from the hen-house.
Would you like to be a farmer?

PIGS

Pigs like to roll in the mud to keep cool. Their skin is delicate and they can get sunburnt!

Pigs will eat almost anything. Many pigs are fed on household scraps.

Pigs can not see very well with their small eyes. They have a big snout and a good sense of smell.

Pigs are very intelligent. Some people even keep them as pets.

Pigs like to scratch their backs against trees or fences.

GOATS

Most goats have horns. The male goat, or billy goat, has a beard.

Goats are very good at climbing. They often graze on steep hillsides.

Goats are kept for their milk. It has a stronger taste than cow's milk.

Angora and Cashmere goats have long soft hair which can be used for making clothes.

Female, or nanny, goats have two or three babies at once. Baby goats are called kids.

SHEEP

Sheep are covered in thick soft wool. We can use this wool to make clothes. We can also use milk from sheep to make delicious cheese.

Male sheep are called rams. Most rams have long, curved horns.

Sheep are kept in large fields. They eat the fresh, green grass. During cold weather farmers feed their sheep on grain and hay.

Lambs are born in the spring. They stay close to their mothers.

CHICKENS

Baby chickens are called chicks. They begin life inside an egg. When they hatch they are covered in soft yellow feathers called down.

Chickens have a fleshy comb on top of their heads. They also have a wattle that hangs below the beak.

Chickens can lay an egg every day. Only a few eggs produce chicks. The rest are good to eat!

Chickens have wings but they can only fly short distances. They sometimes fly up into trees to perch on the branches.

CATS

Farmers often keep cats to get rid of rats and mice which live in their barns and eat the crops.

Cats like to sit on top of walls and rooftops so that they can see what is going on.

Mother cats give birth to their kittens in a quiet corner of the farm. The kittens learn to hunt by copying what their mother does.

Some farm cats may be quite wild and stay away from people. Others make good pets and enjoy the warmth of the farm kitchen!

COWS

Cows are very useful animals. We can make cheese, butter and cream from their milk.

Cows usually give birth to one calf every year. The young calves feed on milk which they suck from their mother's udder.

Cows use their long tails to shoo away insects.

Bulls have large horns and are much bigger than cows.

DUCKS

Ducks have webbed feet which they use like paddles to help them swim.

Ducklings can swim as soon as they are born. They follow their mother into the water.

Ducks like to swim on ponds or streams. They dive down to pick food off the bottom. Their tail feathers stick up in the air.

Ducks have soft feathers which can be used for filling pillows and quilts.

DONKEYS

Donkeys have large heads and long ears. They have short manes and a tuft of hair at the end of their tails.

Donkeys are related to horses but they are smaller and sturdier. They are happy to share a field.

Because donkeys are strong, they can carry heavy loads over rough ground.

A mule is a cross between a horse and a donkey. Mules are very sure-footed. They can be quite stubborn if they are not well-treated.

DOGS

Sheepdogs help farmers herd their flocks of sheep. The dogs are trained not to hurt the sheep.

There are lots of different types of sheepdog. All of them have thick, fur to keep them warm in the snow.

In some countries, farmers keep dogs to protect their sheep from wild animals, such as foxes.

Most farm dogs live outside in kennels, but some are family pets.

FARM QUIZ

Why do farmers keep chickens?

What are baby goats called?

What do you think this cow is doing?

How do cats make themselves useful on the farm?

What do sheep eat in the winter?

What can dogs be trained to do?

What do pigs do if they get an itch?

Have you ever watched ducks on a pond? How do they find food?

INDEX

If you have enjoyed this book look out for the full range

PLAY & DISCOVER • What We Eat • Rain & Shine

CRAFT • Paint • Paper • Fun Food • Dress Up

ANIMALS • Pets • On Safari • Underwater • On the Farm

For more information about TWO-CAN books write to:
Two-Can Publishing Ltd., 346 Old Street, London EC1V 9NQ

First published in Great Britain in 1992 by
Two-Can Publishing Ltd., 346 Old Street, London EC1V 9NQ
in association with Scholastic Publications Ltd

Copyright © Two-Can Publishing Ltd. 1992   Illustration copyright © Siobhan Dodds

Printed and bound in Hong Kong   2 4 6 10 9 7 5 3

The JUMP! logo and the word JUMP! are registered trade marks.

A cataogue record for this book is available from the British Library.

Pbk ISBN 1-85434-147-2
Hbk ISBN 1-85434-152-9

Photo credits: p.2-3 © Fiona Pragoff, p.5 Ardea, p.7 Papilio, p.9 NHPA, p.11 Papilio, p.13 Holt International,
p.15 Oxford Scientific, p.17 Papilio, p.19 Sylvia Cordaiy, p.21 Tony Stone